Empowering

Right-Relationships

Empowering
Right-Relationships

Daniel Henley

Living
Word
Books

Cordova, Tennessee

ISBN: 978-0-9793079-2-8

The Journey Christian Church
1755 Appling Rd
Memphis, TN 38103
www.journeychurchmemphis.org

Living Word Books
Double-Edged Publishing, Inc.
9618 Misty Brook Cove
Cordova, Tennessee 38016

> *For the word of God is living and active. Sharper than any double-edged sword, it penetrates even to dividing soul and spirit, joints and marrow; it judges the thoughts and attitudes of the heart.*

Hebrews 4:12 New International Version (NIV)

www.doubleedgedpublishing.com

Printed in the United States of America
First Printing

Dedication

To the millions of people around the world who are still searching for a "right" relationship with God and with other people. To those who still yearn for more after all the religious ceremonies, customs, traditions and the work has been done. May this book bring comfort to your soul by renewing your mind.

To our God—You get all the honor, all the glory and all the praise. You deserve it.

To Mom and Dad—you are a blessing.

To my wife—I cherish you.

To generational leaders—this book is for you.

To the youth of the world—may your generation never have to struggle through religion to find "right" relationships.

To my dear colleagues and friends at *The Journey Christian Church*—you are truly examples of the spirit of right relationships.

Acknowledgments

This book has taken more than 20 years to prepare, over ten years to contemplate, approximately two years to teach and the efforts of many mentors, teachers, pastors, influencers, family and friends.

To my beloved wife, Dee, you fill me up with your love and support. To my children: Shondra, Dierdre, Danielle and Daniel—you make life fun.

To my natural and spiritual parents—thank you for guiding and directing me for so many years.

To my brother, James, you are the greatest big brother on the planet; and to my sister, Karen—they don't get any better than you.

Special thanks to Pastor Stacy L. Spencer, who has walked so closely with me on my spiritual journey.

To Roy and Carolyn Shirkey, the excellent spirit-writer team and guide in developing this project—you are truly a gift from God and an author's dream team.

To Dr. Reo Pruiett, Dee Moyes, Pastor Larry DeVooght, and my daughter, Dierdre Henley—your editorial support was outstanding.

To my accountability partner and friend, Travis Moody—THANKS!!!

To all the Elders, members and staff of our ministry in Cordova, Tennessee and around the world—thank you for helping us to develop and refine these ideas and concepts by sharing and testing them on you. May you continue to be representatives of God's Kingdom right here on earth.

Empowering
Right-Relationships

Introduction

It is becoming more and more difficult to be a Christian in the twenty-first century. Many people around the world, both Christians and non-Christians, are facing the dilemma of identity. Many people are struggling to discover who they are and where they stand today—in the family, the community, and the world. While many aren't willing to admit it, the struggle does exist.

The questions are typically six-fold:

1. Who is God and what is He really like?
2. Who am I and why am I here?
3. How do I relate to others?
4. What is the will of God for my life?
5. How do I fulfill God's will for my life?
6. What are the benefits?

My wife, D'Juanna, and I have counseled thousands of people in many different situations and the majority of the questions we receive will typically fall into one of these six

1

categories. Though many people are building careers, gaining more and more education, raising families, and participating in their communities—the pace of life is leaving them exhausted and disillusioned. This little book is our humble attempt to try and help answer these questions and more. Enjoy.

-1-

Nature of God-

As a pastor, I am often asked who or what is God. When I am asked this question, I will ask the questioner for his/her description of God. The description given is generally similar to what is depicted in Renaissance paintings. Twenty-first century Americans think of God as a man with flowing white hair and a beard. He has reached out from a place afar, where He is surrounded by a group of blonde haired angels, and has given life to Adam (humankind). He subsequently expels Adam from the Garden of Eden similar to what was painted by Michelangelo on the ceiling of the Sistine Chapel. God is generally described as a God of retribution. However, the real nature of God is Love, Spirit, and Truth.

God is Love. God is Spirit and Truth. God is the source and substance of each one of us. We have heard or read the analogies that God is like a pie and each of us is like a sliver or God is like the ocean and we are like microscopic drops of ocean water. We each have all of the same characteristics as God; yet, God is infinitely great and we are each very small. God's Word says:

In the beginning God created the heavens and the earth. Now the earth was formless and empty, darkness was over the surface of the deep, and the Spirit of God was hovering over the waters (Genesis 1:1-2)[*].

Dear friends, let us love one another, for love comes from God. Everyone who loves has been born of God and knows God. Whoever does not love does not know God, because God is love (1 John 4:7-8).

A time is coming and has now come when the true worshipers will worship the Father in spirit and truth, for they are the kind of worshipers the Father seeks. God is spirit, and his worshipers must worship in spirit and in truth (John 4: 23-24).

God has never stopped revealing Himself. There is the Old Testament, the New Testament and the Now Testament. The Bible is full of examples of God's

---

[*] All Biblical Quotations are from the New International Version (NIV).

revelation. A "revelation" is the act of God revealing or disclosing Himself and His will to humankind. Once the Bible was compiled God did not suddenly withdraw from humankind. God constantly reveals Himself.

God is revealed first and foremost through His son Jesus. God also reveals Himself through His magnificent creations. The earth we live on, the air we breathe, the sun that warms us, the entire litany of marvels which are the creations of God. We also see God in the good works of humankind. Joy, peace, patience, kindness, gentleness, and goodness are attributes, which are often displayed by humankind.

God reveals Himself to each of us individually as a whisper, as a still small voice. God's glory is so great that for us to experience it, He has to cover our faces and turn His back to us for us to be in His presence. God revealed Himself to His prophet Elijah. God said to Elijah "Go out and stand on the mountain in the presence of the LORD, for the LORD is about to pass by." Then a great and powerful wind tore the mountains apart and shattered the rocks before the LORD, but the LORD was not in the wind. After the wind there was an earthquake, but the LORD was not in the earthquake. After the earthquake came a fire, but the LORD was not in the fire. And after the fire came a gentle whisper" (1Kings 19:11-12).

Moses was God's servant and God's friend. God knew Moses by his name. In the Book of Exodus it is recorded where God revealed Himself to Moses:

> And the LORD said to Moses, "I will do the very thing you have asked, because I am pleased with you and I know you by name."
>
> Then Moses said, "Now show me your glory."
>
> And the LORD said, "I will cause all my goodness to pass in front of you, and I will proclaim my name, the LORD, in your presence. I will have mercy on whom I will have mercy, and I will have compassion on whom I will have compassion. But," he said, "you cannot see my face, for no one may see me and live."
>
> Then the LORD said, "There is a place near me where you may stand on a rock. When my glory passes by, I will put you in a cleft in the

rock and cover you with my hand until I have passed by. Then I will remove my hand and you will see my back; but my face must not be seen." (Exodus 33:17-23)

Paul of Tarsus was a Jewish Rabbi and later one of the first great Christian preachers. While the Bible's New Testament consists in large part of letters he wrote, there is little record of his actual sermons. He was a man of his times, as we all are, influenced by the politics, mores, customs and traditions of his time; but, Paul stilled himself and listened to God's revelation.

Paul was a recipient of this revelation. The one record of his preaching dynamics is found in the book of Acts. Paul was in Athens, at a place called Mars Hill. Athens is identified in history books as the birthplace of western civilization. There were a host of gods who were worshiped there and structures erected to facilitate the worship of these gods. Philosophical thinking and debate were an important part of Athenian life.

Paul's entire sermon to the Athenians is only a few sentences long and could not have taken more than a few minutes to deliver:

Paul then stood up in the meeting of the Areopagus and said: "Men of Athens! I see that in every way you are very religious. For as I walked around and looked carefully at your objects of worship, I even found an altar with this inscription: TO AN UNKNOWN GOD. Now what you worship as something unknown I am going to proclaim to you.

"The God who made the world and everything in it is the Lord of heaven and earth and does not live in temples built by hands. And he is not served by human hands, as if he needed anything, because he himself gives all men life and breath and everything else. From one man he made every nation of men, that they should inhabit the whole earth; and he determined the times set for them and the exact places where they should live. God did this so that men would seek him and perhaps reach out for him and find him, though he is not far from each one of us. 'For in him we live and move and have our being.' As some of your own poets have said, 'We are his offspring.'

"Therefore since we are God's offspring, we should not think that the divine being is like gold or silver or stone—an image made by man's design and skill. In the past God overlooked such ignorance, but now he commands all people everywhere to repent. For he has set a day when he will judge the world with justice by the man he has appointed. He has given proof of this to all men by raising him from the dead. (Acts 17:22-31)

As stated by Paul, "From one man he made every nation of men, that they should inhabit the whole earth; and he determined the times set for them and the exact places where they should live. God did this so that men would seek Him and perhaps reach out for him and find him, though he is not far from each one of us" (Acts 17:26-27).

9

The revelation that Paul received is that God designed us to long for Him. We long for God and for a right relationship with Him.

A logical next question might be, what is a right relationship with God? When we think about the best earthly relationships that we have, they are typically the ones that we invest in the most. The relationships that we spend the most time with reap the largest return. God is no different. He longs to spend time with us; however, something is keeping us from spending quality time with God. That something is sin. Since God is such a loving God, He made a way for our sins not to be counted against us; thereby, freeing us to spend all the time that we desire to spend with Him.

The way God accounted for our sins is not complicated. He sent His son Jesus, who had never sinned, to pay for our sins by sacrificing His life for us. The Bible says that while we were still sinners, Jesus died for us. By this one act of a truly righteous person, we all get to enjoy a right relationship with God that is free from the bondage of sin. If we happen to sin, and we probably will from time to time, we ask for forgiveness and continue in our right relationship with God. Wow!!! What a wonderful God we serve!

Jesus was also sent to remind us that God had delivered to humankind through His servant Moses the rules for living, the Ten Commandments[*]. The first four commandments concern how we should conduct our relationship with God, and the remaining six with how we should conduct our relationships with each other. Not one of these commandments states that we should believe in God. We didn't need a commandment like this because God created us so that it is our nature to seek and reach out for Him.

It is a part of the Spiritual design for us to long for a right relationship with God. You can quiet your mind, still yourself, feel your extremities grow heavy and warm, follow your breathing in, as it calms you, and as you exhale, think coolly behind your eyes that God is Love. Concentrate on God as Love. Concentrated prayer such as this can effectively activate some of our dormant Spiritual DNA. Congregational prayer and fasting is even more effective in activating our Spiritual DNA.

---

[*] See Appendix

For example, we at *The Journey Christian Church* (*The Journey*) participate, as a community, in what we call the "5 for 5".

We have agreed to:

1. Pray daily for the 'first' five (5) minutes when we get up;

2. Meditate on five (5) scriptures per day for five minutes (per scripture);

3. Fast and pray at least one day per week from 5 AM to 5 PM (water only; real juice if necessary);

4. Ask God for five (5) things or goals this year that look IMPOSSIPLE;

5. Ask God to help us identify five (5) people and/or things that will hinder our plans for this year and do two things:

   a. Cut them off!!!

   b. Replace them with positive people (Believers) and/or things.

We aren't all "religious" about this. There won't be severe consequences if we fail to adhere to the "5 for 5."

Our goal is as a Spiritual community of believers to collectively activate our Spiritual DNA. God is the source and substance of each of us. We all share this Spiritual DNA.

It doesn't take much for you to feel and know that fundamentally you are the same substance, by nature, as God. It is more difficult to look into the face of others and know they share the same Spiritual DNA as you and are fundamentally the same substance as God. This is especially true if they don't look much like you in the mirror. If they are a different sex, have a different skin and hair color, hair texture, nationality, ethnicity, religion, sexual preference than you, do you see that they too are the same substance as God?

Spirit and Truth is like the wind. It flows from and into each of us who have a tender heart. As a congregation through God and through Jesus we seek to tenderize hearts.

Since God is the source and substance of each one of us we, at *The Journey,* are deliberately and intentionally a multi-racial church. A multi-racial church, by definition, is a church where no more than 80% of its members are of the same race. For example, if a church consists of 79% white members and 21% black and Latinos members, it is by definition a multi-racial church. While we use the term multi-racial because it is commonly used in describing churches, we actually don't believe in race. Race is a myth created by humankind and is designed to keep the body of Christ divided. We believe that each individual is like a piece of glass in a great stained glass creation that God has made. Each individual piece of glass irrespective of its nature, whether it is jagged, smooth, large or small, black, brown, red, yellow, or white is just as significant, just as important as the other in God's creation, plan and purpose.

The last prayer that Jesus prayed before His crucifixion and resurrection is a revelation:

> My prayer is not for them alone. I pray also for those who will believe in me through their message, that all of them may be one, Father, just as you are in me and I am in you. May they also be in us so that the world may believe that you have sent me. I have given them the glory that you gave me, that they may be one as we are one: I in them and you in me. May

they be brought to complete unity to let the world know that you sent me and have loved them even as you have loved me. "Father, I want those you have given me to be with me where I am, and to see my glory, the glory you have given me because you loved me before the creation of the world. "Righteous Father, though the world does not know you, I know you, and they know that you have sent me. I have made you known to them, and will continue to make you known in order that the love you have for me may be in them and that I myself may be in them (John 17:20-26).

We became Christians through the message of Jesus' disciples. This prayer is, therefore, specifically for us. Jesus prayed that we be one with our Father and one with each other so that the world may believe that Jesus was sent by the Father.

God's creation, plan, and purpose, which Jesus prayed that it come to fruition, was for each of us, whether we are jagged, smooth, large or small, black, brown, red, yellow, or white, to become one with our Father and each other.

15

Our Lord and Savior Jesus, the Anointed One, came to make the way and show the way, to give us the opportunity, after the fall of humankind in the Garden of Eden, to come again into a right relationship with God.

When we ask ourselves who is God and what is He really like, we should answer that He is Love, Spirit, and Truth. The Truth is that those of us who have become Christians through the message of Jesus' disciples must be brought to complete unity to show the world that God sent Jesus and God loves all of humankind as He loves Jesus. Jesus ended His prayer to God, praying, "I have made you known to them, and will continue to make you known in order that the love you have for me may be in them and that I myself may be in them" (John 17:26). The nature of God is indeed Love, Spirit, and Truth.

$$\Omega$$

Empowering Right Relationships:
First to God, Then to Each Other

Principles:

1. God is Love. God is Spirit and Truth.

2. God has never stopped revealing Himself. There is the Old Testament, the New Testament, and the Now Testament.

3. We long for God and for a right relationship with Him. God designed us to long for Him.

4. Race is a myth created by humankind and is designed to keep the body of Christ divided.

5. Jesus prayed that we would be one with our Father and with each other, so that the world would believe that He was sent by the Father.

6. The nature of God is indeed Love, Spirit, and Truth.

17

-2-

Nature of Humankind-

When I was grounded in the secular world, I had a lust problem and was a "functional" alcoholic. I tried as hard as I could to stop both habits, which continually lead to bad results. While I am glad to report that I have been delivered from both addictions, it wasn't until I got this teaching that my life changed dramatically.

Human beings are three-part beings. They have Spirit, soul, and body.

God's Word says:

> Be joyful always; pray continually; give thanks in all circumstances, for this is God's will for you in Christ Jesus.
>
> Do not put out the Spirit's fire; do not treat prophecies with contempt. Test everything. Hold on to the good. Avoid every kind of evil.

> May God himself, the God of peace, sanctify you through and through.
>
> May your whole spirit, soul and body be kept blameless at the coming of our Lord Jesus Christ. (1Thessalonians 5:16-23)

God through Jesus became flesh and walked on this earth among humankind. He talked, ate, drank, and interacted with human beings. He was also tempted. He experienced happiness; He also experienced sadness. Jesus on this earth, in the flesh, had all of the traits and all of the nature that comes with the human body. Jesus as human also had all of God's nature: Love, Spirit, and Truth. God through Jesus in this fleshly form was a one-time event, a supernatural event, with a specific purpose, which changed the world. Jesus made the opportunity for humankind to come again into a right relationship with God.

Human beings have a body, an earth suit. This is the most obvious part of our being. With this body come fleshly needs: water; food for sustenance; wants for comfort; wants for pleasure—the entire pyramid of needs and wants from the basic to the ridiculous.

A body with needs makes us an animal. Scientists are in the process of mapping the human genome. A genome is the complete collection of an organism's genetic material. The human genome is composed of thousands of genes located on the 23 pairs of chromosomes in a human cell. Scientists will be able to do miraculous things with this knowledge, having a better understanding of how this earth suit works. However, an extremely large percentage of this human genetic material is identical to a chimpanzee or a dust mite.

We are more than animals who have a body. We also possess a soul. The soul is our essence as individuals. It is our uniqueness, our individuality. The soul is what we are born with, what we are taught, what we learn, and our life experiences. Our soul functions through our mind (thinker), emotions (feeler), and our will (chooser). The psalmist decreed that He restores our soul. What is God restoring when He restores a soul? He restores our soul with zest, zeal and enthusiasm for life.

As God is Spirit, we also are spirit. We can only grasp and glimpse a very small piece of Spirit. It is fire; it is glory; it is the universal energy that is the source and substance of everything. "Do not put out the Spirit's fire" (1 Thessalonians 5:19).

God is Love, as a noun, as part of His nature; He is also Love in action, as a verb. He acts with love that is unconditional. He pours the oil on our heads that runs down through our hair, oozes down our bodies, and is absorbed into our pours. It soothes us. It heals us. He gives us a glass of water, which drips down our chin as we drink it. It cools us. It invigorates us. God takes care of humankind's body and soul because He loves us unconditionally.

As God is Love, we are also Love in action. We were created in the image of God and God has poured out His Love into our hearts, by His Spirit. As believers, we have God (His Spirit) inside of us and therefore, we can love others as God would have us to. Paul says, "And hope does not disappoint us, because God has poured out his love into our hearts by the Holy Spirit, whom he has given us" (Romans 5:6). While this is a great truth that begs for our attention; it is my contention that most believers have missed this fundamental teaching. God, who is Love, lives inside of us. And since God, who is Love, lives inside of us; we too can love like God.

Imagine a glass pitcher or a clear container that is full of water. Then imagine an empty glass right beside the pitcher on a table. If you were to pick up the glass pitcher and pour the water that's inside it into the empty glass, the glass would then contain the exact same substance as the pitcher...water. God is no different. He took from Himself, His Love, and poured it into our hearts and we now contain the exact same substance as God...Love. Therefore, it bears repeating that God, who is Love, lives inside of us. And since God, who is Love, lives inside of us; we too can love like God.

Jesus functioned on earth as a three-part being. He differed from us as human beings in that He was able to totally reject, as having no authority or binding force, His body and His soul and live each moment in Spirit. As He walked through the crowd, a young woman touched His clothes and absorbed Spirit. This wasn't through a willful act of Jesus. He didn't turn on some spigot and let Spirit loose. He radiates Spirit even today; only today, He radiates Spirit through us.

As human beings we operate within all three parts simultaneously. We are of Spirit, we possess a soul and we live in a physical body. None of us certainly lives each moment in Spirit; but that is our longing. We long to be near and close to God and this is only found in Spirit.

Jesus took hold of one of these earth suits to make and then show us the way of the Lord, which is Love. He came to put us again in a right relationship with God. His teaching was simple; His example profound. If you cut out of the Bible all of the red ink teachings of Jesus and pasted them in a publication, it would be no larger than a magazine without the advertisements.

However, His teachings are more powerful than all of the great books of humankind combined.

Human beings understand the life and teachings of the historical Jesus. He was sent by God. He lived a blameless life, loved, performed miracles, was killed on a tree and arose from the dead. Christians have faith that this is true. Christians believe as Jesus taught

I am the true vine, and my Father is the gardener. He cuts off every branch in me that bears no fruit, while every branch that does bear fruit he prunes so that it will be even more

24

fruitful. You are already clean because of the word I have spoken to you. Remain in me, and I will remain in you. No branch can bear fruit by itself; it must remain in the vine. Neither can you bear fruit unless you remain in me. (John 15:1-4)

Jesus also taught:

As the Father has loved me, so have I loved you. Now remain in my love. If you obey my commands, you will remain in my love, just as I have obeyed my Father's commands and remain in his love. I have told you this so that my joy may be in you and that your joy may be complete. My command is this: Love each other as I have loved you. (John 15: 9-12)

Jesus was tested by a man well educated in man's laws and man's traditions. This man was what Jesus would describe as a wolf in sheep's clothing. He was not attempting to discern Jesus' teachings, but was attempting to carry out the desires of his father, Satan. Jesus had said,

25

concerning Satan, "He was a murderer from the beginning; not holding to the truth, for there is no truth in him. When he lies, he speaks his native language, for he is a liar and the father of lies" (John 8:44). This wolf in sheep's clothing asked Jesus, "Teacher, which is the greatest commandment in the Law?"

Jesus replied: "Love the Lord your God with all your heart and with all your soul and with all your mind. This is the first and greatest commandment. And the second is like it: Love your neighbor as yourself. All the Law and the Prophets hang on these two commandments" (Matthew 22:36-40).

Jesus taught us if we love Him, we will obey His commandments. Fundamentally, these are the only two commandments that Jesus gave us:

> 1. We should love God with our whole heart, soul and mind. Love as a noun and also love as an action.
>
> 2. We should love our neighbor as ourselves, as a noun and as an action.

By doing just these two commandments, we are loving with our entire three-part being. Our Spirit and soul are loving God; which in turn allows an outward expression of love, through our earthly bodies, to our neighbors. But some might ask, "Who is our neighbor?" Is it our friends, our relatives, others who look like us in the mirror? Jesus' parable of the Good Samaritan is a revelation:

> On one occasion an expert in the law stood up to test Jesus. "Teacher," he asked, "what must I do to inherit eternal life?"
>
> "What is written in the Law?" he replied. "How do you read it?"
>
> He answered: "'Love the Lord your God with all your heart and with all your soul and with all your strength and with all your mind'; and, 'Love your neighbor as yourself.'"
>
> "You have answered correctly," Jesus replied. "Do this and you will live."
>
> But he wanted to justify himself, so he asked Jesus, "And who is my neighbor?"
>
> In reply Jesus said: "A man was going down from Jerusalem to Jericho, when he fell

into the hands of robbers. They stripped him of his clothes, beat him and went away, leaving him half dead. A priest happened to be going down the same road, and when he saw the man, he passed by on the other side. So too, a Levite, when he came to the place and saw him, passed by on the other side. But a Samaritan, as he traveled, came where the man was; and when he saw him, he took pity on him. He went to him and bandaged his wounds, pouring on oil and wine. Then he put the man on his own donkey, took him to an inn and took care of him. The next day he took out two silver coins and gave them to the innkeeper. 'Look after him,' he said, 'and when I return, I will reimburse you for any extra expense you may have.'

"Which of these three do you think was a neighbor to the man who fell into the hands of robbers?"

The expert in the law replied, "The one who had mercy on him."

Jesus told him, "Go and do likewise." (Luke 10 25-37)

Jesus was speaking to a Jew, who was an expert on man's laws and traditions. The individual Jesus told the expert to love was a Samaritan, a mixed race of Jew and other nationalities; a race that historians say was despised by the Jews. This is probably why when Jesus asked which man was a neighbor to the man who fell into the hands of robbers, the expert in the law couldn't even say "the Samaritan"; instead he answered, "the one who had mercy on him." Jesus' second commandment is for us to love all other human beings irrespective of the nature of their bodies and their souls. We are to love each other whether we are jagged, smooth, large or small, black, brown, red, yellow, or white.

When we are asked who we are, we should respond confidently that we are Spirit, soul, and body. When we are asked why we are here, we should respond confidently that it is to adhere to Jesus' commandments and there are fundamentally only two: (1) we are to love God with every fiber of our Spirit, souls and bodies and (2) we are to love each other irrespective of the nature of our souls and bodies. This is the mission we have at *The Journey*, obeying Jesus' commandments. We can attest that the rewards of following these two very simple, yet profound, commandments are extraordinary.

Ω

Empowering Right Relationships:
First to God, Then to Each Other

Principles:

1. Human beings are three-part beings. We are Spirit, we possess a soul and we live in a physical body.

2. A body with needs makes us an animal.

3. We are more than animals who have a body. We also possess a soul.

4. As God is Spirit, we also are Spirit.

5. God is Love, as a noun, as part of His nature; He is also Love in action, as a verb.

6. Jesus taught us if we love Him, we will obey His two basic commandments:

    a. We should love God with our whole heart, soul and mind. Love as a noun and also love as an action.

    b. We should love our neighbor as ourselves, as a noun and as an action.

7. God, who is Love, lives inside of us. Since God, who is Love, lives inside of us, we too can love like God.

-3-

Borders-

Poet and clergyman John Donne (1572-1631) lyrically described within his 27th meditation how human beings relate to each other. "All mankind is of one author, and is one volume; when one man dies, one chapter is not torn out of the book, but translated into a better language; and every chapter must be so translated... As therefore the bell that rings to a sermon, calls not upon the preacher only, but upon the congregation to come: so this bell calls us all... No man is an island, entire of itself...any man's death diminishes me, because I am involved in mankind; and therefore never send to know for whom the bell tolls; it tolls for thee."

I had a personal education on how I relate to others when, as a divinity student, I participated in a mission trip to Mexico. This was a life changing experience.

The border between Mexico and the United States is like the border between the haves and the have-nots.

We stayed as guests in the home of a family. They lived under conditions, which at best would be called abject poverty. Only the mother attended church, although the entire family was a Christian family. One of the sons could speak some English and served as a translator.

The mother had a question, which she said she had asked her pastor but he could not answer. She wanted to know, "What is this power called faith?" She knew the Bible said that with faith you can move mountains. What exactly was this powerful substance?

Most students of the Bible are familiar with Paul's description of faith, "Now faith is being sure of what we hope for and certain of what we do not see" (Hebrews 11:1). When I responded to the mother's question, my tongue was moved to say, "Faith is the Word of God."

We are reminded, over and over again, in scripture that, "Man does not live on bread alone, but on every word that comes from the mouth of God" (Matthew 3:4). We can move mountains through the Word of God!

Looking at Hebrews 11, the phrase the "Word of God" can be substituted for the word faith as follows: By the

Word of God—Abel[*] offered God a better sacrifice than Cain did. By the Word of God he was commended as a righteous man.

By the Word of God—Enoch[*] was taken from this life, so that he did not experience death; he could not be found, because God had taken him away. For before he was taken, he was commended as one who pleased God.

By the Word of God—Noah[*] when warned about things not yet seen, in holy fear built an ark to save his family. By the Word of God he condemned the world and became heir of the righteousness that comes by the Word of God.

By the Word of God—Abraham[*] when called to go to a place he would later receive as his inheritance, obeyed and went, even though he did not know where he was going. By the Word of God he made his home in the Promised Land like a stranger in a foreign country; he lived in tents, as did Isaac and Jacob, who were heirs with him of the same promise. For he was looking forward to the city with foundations, whose architect and builder is God.

---

[*] See Appendix.

<u>By the Word of God</u>—Abraham, even though he was past age—and Sarah herself was barren—was enabled to become a father.

<u>By the Word of God</u>—Abraham, when God tested him, offered Isaac as a sacrifice.

<u>By the Word of God</u>—Isaac* blessed Jacob and Esau in regard to their future.

<u>By the Word of God</u>—Jacob*, when he was dying, blessed each of Joseph's sons, and worshiped as he leaned on the top of his staff.

<u>By the Word of God</u>—Joseph*, when his end was near, spoke about the exodus of the Israelites from Egypt and gave instructions about his bones.

<u>By the Word of God</u>—Moses'* parents hid him for three months after he was born, because they saw he was no ordinary child, and they were not afraid of the king's edict.

<u>By the Word of God</u>—Moses, when he had grown up, refused to be known as the son of Pharaoh's daughter. He chose to be mistreated along with the people of God rather than to enjoy the pleasures of sin for a short time. He regarded disgrace for the sake of Christ as of greater value than the treasures of Egypt, because he was looking ahead

to his reward. <u>By the Word of God</u> he left Egypt, not fearing the king's anger; he persevered because he saw him who is invisible. <u>By the Word of God</u> he kept the Passover and the sprinkling of blood, so that the destroyer of the firstborn would not touch the firstborn of Israel.

<u>By the Word of God</u>—the people passed through the Red Sea as on dry land; but when the Egyptians tried to do so, they were drowned.

<u>By the Word of God</u>—the walls of Jericho fell, after the people had marched around them for seven days.

<u>By the Word of God</u>—the prostitute Rahab[*], because she welcomed the spies, was not killed with those who were disobedient.

Abel, Enoch, Noah, Abraham, Sarah, Jacob, Issac, Rahab, and all the other people mentioned above are all just that...people. They were ordinary people that God used to do extraordinary things. We are no different today. By the Word of God, we too can move or, better yet, remove the current day mountains. You know the mountain of lust or alcoholism, as it was in my case. Or maybe your mountain is drugs, sexual immorality, homosexuality, racism,

---

[*] See Appendix.

idolatry, adultery, lying, gossiping, stealing, and the list goes on and on. It doesn't matter, because the answer is the same; we move mountains by the Word of God.

We also learn that the only way to remove the borders, whether apparent or invisible, between families, between females and males, between races, between nationalities, between ethnicities, between religions, and between individuals with different sexual preferences is also by the Word of God.

The Word of God (faith) is the universal source and substance of everything. "In the beginning was the Word, and the Word was with God, and the Word was God. He was with God in the beginning. Through him all things were made; without him nothing was made that has been made" (John 1:1-3).

The Word of God (faith) is the power by which we can move mountains. How do we acquire this faith? We acquire this faith through absorption of the Word of God through our ears, our eyes, and letting it roll off our tongues. "So then faith comes by hearing, and hearing by the Word of God" (Romans 10:17).

As we acquire this faith or the Word of God, we began to view the world differently. For example, in the secular world, I received a lesson in the concept of "we." I was a representative for a Japanese computer company and was negotiating a deal with a large American company. In a meeting I used the term "we." A member of the American company stopped me and asked me, "Who is we?" In my mind initially I thought of "we" as me and the Japanese company I was representing. I learned that the "we" was both the Japanese and American companies and how "we," the Japanese company, could work to help solve the American company's problems.

Similarly, *The Journey* is a Reconciliation Church. To reconcile is to join back together what God intended to be together before we were divided and separated by the laws and the traditions of men. To do this, we must redefine the word, "we."

"We" is not we Asians, Blacks, Latinos, Whites; not we females and we males. "We" is we Christians. Jesus was preaching to a large crowd. His mother and brother came to see Him; but they could not get to Him because of the crowd. Someone got Jesus' attention and told Him that

His mother and brothers wanted to see Him. Jesus' response was, "My mother and brothers are those who hear God's word and put it into practice" (Luke 8:19-21). "We," Christians, are those who hear God's Word and put them into practice.

Inside Jesus' parable of the Shrewd Manager is a revelation of the Word of God:

> Jesus told his disciples: "There was a rich man whose manager was accused of wasting his possessions. So he called him in and asked him, 'What is this I hear about you? Give an account of your management, because you cannot be manager any longer.'
>
> "The manager said to himself, 'What shall I do now? My master is taking away my job. I'm not strong enough to dig, and I'm ashamed to beg. I know what I'll do so that, when I lose my job here, people will welcome me into their houses.'
>
> "So he called in each one of his master's debtors. He asked the first, 'How much do you owe my master?'

"'Eight hundred gallons of olive oil,' he replied.

"The manager told him, 'Take your bill, sit down quickly, and make it four hundred.'

"Then he asked the second, 'And how much do you owe?

"'A thousand bushels of wheat,' he replied.

"He told him, 'Take your bill and make it eight hundred.'

"The master commended the dishonest manager because he had acted shrewdly. For the people of this world are more shrewd in dealing with their own kind than are the people of the light. I tell you, use worldly wealth to gain friends for yourselves, so that when it is gone, you will be welcomed into eternal dwellings." (Luke 16:1-9)

"For the people of this world are more shrewd in dealing with their own kind than are *[we]* the people of the light." In the secular world, I understood and used the concept of "we" to acquire worldly wealth. However, "we" as Christians, the people of the light, must understand the

Spiritual "we" to gain Spiritual wealth. Worldly wealth is good, but Spiritual wealth is better, as we will examine in Chapter 6.

Like the border between Mexico and the United States, there are borders, some apparent and some invisible, between females and males, between races, between nationalities, between ethnicities, between religions, and between individuals with different sexual preferences. "We" Christians do not have borders among ourselves. We know that all mankind is of one author, and is one volume; the bell that rings to a sermon calls not upon the preacher only, but upon the congregation to come. So this bell calls us all; no man is an island, entire in itself. Any person's death diminishes us all, because "we" Christians are all involved in mankind. God holds us accountable for how we relate or fail to relate to all our sisters and brothers in Christ.

Ω

Empowering Right Relationships:
First to God, Then to Each Other

Principles:

1. We can move mountains through the Word of God.

2. We must learn to redefine the word "we." "We" is not we Asians, Blacks, Latinos, Whites; not we females or we males. "We" is we Christians.

3. "We," Christians, are those who hear God's Word and put them into practice.

4. "We" Christians, do not have borders among ourselves.

5. Worldly wealth is good, but Spiritual wealth is better.

43

-4-

Vision, Dry Bones, Watchman-

Now we enter into the question, "What is the will of God for my life?" A good place to start is where God started. In the beginning there was a void. From the void, God created the unseen (heavens) where He resides, and the seen (earth) over which He gave dominion to us, females and males. God's purpose for each of our lives is for us to utilize the unique gifts which He has given us. He has given them in abundance to take dominion over the seen, that is, to serve as the hand's of God on earth to ensure that His will and His Kingdom is on this earth as it is in Heaven. God's will is that we have a right relationship with Him and with each other.

God revealed to one of the ancient prophets: "I will pour out my Spirit on all people. Your sons and daughters will prophesy, your old men will dream dreams, your young men will see visions" (Joel 2:28).

When the Holy Spirit came at Pentecost, Jesus' disciple, Peter, proclaimed: "In the last days, God says, I will pour out my Spirit on all people. Your sons and daughters will prophesy, your young men will see visions, your old men will dream dreams. Even on my servants, both men and women, I will pour out my Spirit in those days, and they will prophesy. I will show wonders in the heaven above and signs on the earth below, blood and fire and billows of smoke. The sun will be turned to darkness and the moon to blood before the coming of the great and glorious day of the Lord. And everyone who calls on the name of the Lord will be saved" (Acts 2:17-21).

As previously stated, human beings are three-part beings. We are Spirit. We possess a soul and we live in an earthly body. Everyone understands the needs of the human body. Instinctively a newborn baby suckles on the mother's breast. We all know we need food, water, clothing, and shelter.

As we discussed in chapter two, the soul, the essence of the individual, is more complicated. Scientists have determined the human genome is composed of roughly 20,000 genes located on the 23 pairs of chromosomes in a human cell. On one of these chromosomes, scientists estimate there are more than 250 million DNA base pairs, and scientists estimate that the entire human genome consists of about 3 billion base pairs. In the human body, these 3 billion pairs of genetic material make us human. Obviously, the soul is significantly more complex than the body. The soul is the sum of our personal uniqueness. It consists of what we are born with, what we are taught, what we learn, and our life experiences.

We are born with characteristics which society associates with female or male. This is very different from socialized female and male characteristics, where certain dress, hairstyle, and demeanor are expected of the sexes by man's laws and traditions.

Not all females have all of the characteristics that society associates with femininity. Not all males have all of the characteristics that society associates with masculinity. It is not uncommon for females or males to have characteristics that society associates with the opposite sex. We are each unique. If there are 3 billion pairs of the genetic material, which makes up the unique human body, there are an infinitely greater number of characteristics, which are associated with the soul.

But the soul is even more complex. We have all been taught differently and we all learn differently. We each also have different life experiences. Each soul is individual and unique. It is in the soul where free will and self-destination exists.

While our souls are unique, they all function in the same manner. Souls function through the mind (thinker), the emotions (feeler) and the will (chooser). The complex soul functions in a simple, straightforward manner. If we think about a certain subject, our feelings will consist of what we are thinking and our desires and corresponding actions will be driven by what we are thinking. This process works irrespective of the circumstance.

The process works like this. Two individuals have been laid off their jobs. One thinks this a tragedy, something bad has happened. As one thinks, so follows feelings and then actions. The other thinks this is a marvelous opportunity for self-development and expansion. Again, as one thinks so follows feelings and then actions. If you check your feelings and you feel sad, angry, or happy, you will find that you are thinking sad, angry or happy thoughts and your actions will follow accordingly.

Paul of Tarsus advised, "Do not conform any longer to the pattern of this world, but be transformed by the renewing of your mind. Then you will be able to test and approve what God's will is—his good, pleasing and perfect will" (Romans 12:2). God purposes us to serve as His hands on earth to ensure that His will (we have a right relationship with Him and each other) and His Kingdom is on this earth as it is in Heaven.

"Whatever is true, whatever is noble, whatever is right, whatever is pure, whatever is lovely, whatever is admirable—if anything is excellent or praiseworthy—think about such things" (Philippians 4:8). As we renew our minds, our feelings and actions correspond to the mind's renewal. Doing the will of God on this earth is what is noble, right, pure, lovely, admirable, excellent, and praiseworthy.

What is the relationship of Spirit, the universal energy that is the source and substance of everything, to the soul and body? Innately, we all have a longing, a craving for

God. Our souls and bodies desire completeness with God, a right relationship with God.

The completeness of soul and body with Spirit, the coming into a right relationship with God comes through Jesus Christ and it comes in the present moment, in the right now. As God has neither beginning nor end and is always the same, every moment for God is right now.

God is infinite. As far back as your mind can comprehend, as measured by a man made clock, past your birth, your parents birth, your grandparents birth, on and on and well beyond, God exists. As you think forward in the future, well beyond what you can comprehend, God is there. "Jesus Christ is the same yesterday and today and forever" (Hebrews 13:8).

Jesus was asked about the coming of the Kingdom of God. He replied, "The kingdom of God does not come with your careful observation, nor will people say, 'Here it is,' or 'There it is,' because the kingdom of God is within you" (Luke 17:20). The Kingdom of God is within us, right now, at this present moment.

Many of us are prevented from stepping forward into this present moment Kingdom because we serve gods other than our Perfect Father. God's commandment says:

"You shall have no other gods before me. You shall not make for yourself an idol in the form of anything in heaven above or on the earth beneath or in the waters below. You shall not bow down to them or worship them; for I, the LORD your God, am a jealous God, punishing the children for the sin of the fathers to the third and fourth generation of those who hate me, but showing love to a thousand {generations} of those who love me and keep my commandments." (Exodus 20:4-6)

Each of us has had or has seen examples of present moment experiences, where the individual is so consumed in the present moment that all concerns and cares of the world are forgotten and the absorption in the activity is so complete, there is no concern about the ultimate outcome of the activity. You have seen Michel Jordan with a basketball in the zone, in the flow; Tiger Woods with a golf

51

club in the zone, in the flow. Indeed, as fans, we can become absorbed in the present moment of a football or basketball game, as if we were seeking the nearness and closeness of the football and basketball god.

We can have as gods and idols: exceptional corporate, athletic, artistic performance, etc. We can even have present moment experiences induced through drugs, alcohol, and sexual activities. These are examples of worshiping false gods. I was induced by these false gods. I attempted to find present moment experiences through corporate performances, alcohol, and sexual activities. This was nothing but idolatry.

It was only through Jesus Christ and through His instructions regarding prayer, meditation, fasting, hearing God's Word and putting it into practice, that I came into nearness and closeness with God. I then began to experience the joy of knowing I had a right relationship with God, and He began to reveal His will for my life.

The awesomeness of a right relationship with God is extraordinary. We become the fruit of Spirit, which is love, joy, peace, patience, kindness, goodness, faithfulness, gentleness and self-control (Galatians 5:22). We act based upon intuition, conscience, and the spark of God, rather than our emotions and feelings through what we were born with, what we were taught, what we have learned, and our life experiences. God knows and speaks your name and you can experience divine revelation directly through your relationship with Him.

Jesus asked His disciples,

"Who do people say the Son of Man is?"

They replied, "Some say John the Baptist; others say Elijah; and still others, Jeremiah or one of the prophets."

But what about you?" he asked. "Who do you say I am?"

Simon Peter answered, "You are the Christ, the Son of the living God."

Jesus replied, "Blessed are you, Simon son of Jonah, for this was not revealed to you by man, but by my Father in heaven. And I tell you that you are Peter, and on this rock I will build my church, and the gates of Hades will not overcome it. I will give you the keys of the kingdom of heaven; whatever you bind on

53

earth will be bound in heaven, and whatever you loose on earth will be loosed in heaven." (Matthew 16:13-19)

It was revealed to Simon Peter by God that Jesus is the Son of the Living God. He did not deduce this through anything he was taught or had learned or experienced through his life; it was a revelation. Jesus said this is how His church would be built. The church will be built on the same thing that happened to Peter- revealed knowledge, from God to us. God is still in the revealing business.

There is the Old Testament, the New Testament and the Now Testament. The church is built on revelation knowledge. And since we, as Christians, are the church, our lives are built on revealed knowledge from God, directly to us.

Martha, another follower of Jesus, had the same revelation. Jesus said to Martha, "I am the resurrection and the life. He who believes in me will live, even though he dies; and whoever lives and believes in me will never die. Do you believe this?"

"Yes, Lord," she told him, "I believe that you are the Christ, the Son of God, who was to come into the world" (John 11:25-27).

The true nature of Jesus was made known to Peter and to Martha through revelation. Jesus went on to convey to us that upon this revelation of who He is, also comes the reward of the keys to the Kingdom of heaven. The keys to the Kingdom are revealed knowledge from God directly to us. These keys unlock the true riches of the glory of God, which is His Anointing. And these riches are available for anyone who truly believes that Jesus is the Christ; the Son of the Living God. We each come to know what is the will of God in our lives through revelation knowledge from God.

The initial Christians were Jews, as was Jesus. The Jewish nation believed that it alone of all nations was blessed by God. The first Christians believed that Jesus had come to put the Jewish nation back into a right relationship with God.

Jesus came to make the way and show the way for all humankind to come again into a right relationship with God. This was revealed to Peter, as he described:

…"I was in the city of Joppa praying, and in a trance I saw a vision. I saw something like a large sheet being let down from heaven by its four corners, and it came down to where I was. I looked into it and saw four-footed animals of the earth, wild beasts, reptiles, and birds of the air. Then I heard a voice telling me, 'Get up, Peter. Kill and eat.'

"I replied, 'Surely not, Lord! Nothing impure or unclean has ever entered my mouth.'

"The voice spoke from heaven a second time, 'Do not call anything impure that God has made clean.' This happened three times, and then it was all pulled up to heaven again.

"Right then three men who had been sent to me from Caesarea stopped at the house where I was staying. The Spirit told me to have no hesitation about going with them. These six brothers also went with me, and we entered the man's house. He told us how he had seen an angel appear in his house and say, 'Send to

Joppa for Simon who is called Peter. He will bring you a message through which you and all your household will be saved.'

"As I began to speak, the Holy Spirit came on them as he had come on us at the beginning. Then I remembered what the Lord had said: 'John baptized with water, but you will be baptized with the Holy Spirit.' So if God gave them the same gift as he gave us, who believed in the Lord Jesus Christ, who was I to think that I could oppose God?" (Acts 11:5-17)

As Peter stated, "So if God gave them the same gift as he gave us, who believed in the Lord Jesus Christ, who was I to think that I could oppose God?" Racism, sexism, chauvinism and national xenophobia (an unreasonable fear or hatred of foreigners) are all oppositions to God. We must have the right understanding of "we." We must take the journey of reconciliation. We must join back together what God intended to be together before we were divided and separated by the laws and the traditions of men.

My personal revelation from God is that I am to teach and guide a reconciliation ministry. I was drawn into the

57

fire and I saw how the words of the prophet Ezekiel were to apply to me. Ezekiel, Chapter 3 reads:

> "He then said to me: "Son of man, go now to the house of Israel and speak my words to them. You are not being sent to a people of obscure speech and difficult language, but to the house of Israel- not to many peoples of obscure speech and difficult language, whose words you cannot understand. Surely if I had sent you to them, they would have listened to you. But the house of Israel is not willing to listen to you because they are not willing to listen to me, for the whole house of Israel is hardened and obstinate. But I will make you as unyielding and hardened as they are. I will make your forehead like the hardest stone, harder than flint. Do not be afraid of them or terrified by them, though they are a rebellious house." (Ezekiel 3:4-9)

God said to speak His words to the people. I am not being sent to a people of obscure speech and difficult language. They can understand, but they are not willing to listen to me because they are not willing to listen to God. The people have hardened and obstinate hearts for they have been divided and separated by the laws and traditions of men. But I am as unyielding and hardened as they are. God imparted upon me a vision and mission of a reconciliation ministry similar to what was laid upon Ezekiel by the hand of the Lord. This is God's will for my life. God reemphasized this to me when I was in a sabbatical of prayer, meditation and fasting. I was drawn to Ezekiel, Chapter 37:

> The hand of the LORD was upon me, and he brought me out by the Spirit of the LORD and set me in the middle of a valley; it was full of bones. He led me back and forth among them, and I saw a great many bones on the floor of the valley, bones that were very dry. He asked me, "Son of man, can these bones live?"
>
> I said, "O Sovereign LORD, you alone know."

Then he said to me, "Prophesy to these bones and say to them, 'Dry bones, hear the word of the LORD! This is what the Sovereign LORD says to these bones: I will make breath enter you, and you will come to life. I will attach tendons to you and make flesh come upon you and cover you with skin; I will put breath in you, and you will come to life. Then you will know that I am the LORD.' "

So I prophesied as I was commanded. And as I was prophesying, there was a noise, a rattling sound, and the bones came together, bone to bone. I looked, and tendons and flesh appeared on them and skin covered them, but there was no breath in them.

Then he said to me, "Prophesy to the breath; prophesy, son of man, and say to it, 'This is what the Sovereign LORD says: Come from the four winds, O breath, and breathe into these slain, that they may live.' "So I prophesied as he commanded me, and breath entered them; they came to life and stood up on their feet—a vast army.

Then he said to me: "Son of man, these bones are the whole house of Israel. They say, 'Our bones are dried up and our hope is gone; we are cut off.' Therefore prophesy and say to them: 'This is what the Sovereign LORD says: O my people, I am going to open your graves and bring you up from them; I will bring you back to the land of Israel. Then you, my people, will know that I am the LORD, when I open your graves and bring you up from them. I will put my Spirit in you and you will live, and I will settle you in your own land. Then you will know that I the LORD have spoken, and I have done it, declares the LORD.' " (Ezekiel 37:1-14)

The purpose of God for my life is to be a minister of a reconciliation ministry. This is my individual assignment in ensuring that God's will and Kingdom is done on this earth. We each have gifts that we are to apply to this purpose. As was noted by Paul of Tarsus:

"For by the grace given me I say to every one of you: Do not think of yourself more highly than you ought, but rather think of yourself with sober judgment, in accordance with the measure of faith God has given you. Just as each of us has one body with many members, and these members do not all have the same function, so in Christ we who are many form one body, and each member belongs to all the others. We have different gifts, according to the grace given us. If a man's gift is prophesying, let him use it in proportion to his faith. If it is serving, let him serve; if it is teaching, let him teach; if it is encouraging, let him encourage; if it is contributing to the needs of others, let him give generously; if it is leadership, let him govern diligently; if it is showing mercy, let him do it cheerfully." (Romans 12: 3-8)

Ω

Empowering Right Relationships:
First to God, Then to Each Other

Principles:

1. Human beings are three-part beings. We are Spirit, we possess a soul and we live in an earth suit that we call a body.

2   The soul is the sum of our personal uniqueness. It consists of what we're born with, what we are taught, what we learn and our life experiences.

3   While our souls are unique, they all function in the same manner. Souls function through:

   a. The mind (thinker)
   b. The emotions (feeler)
   c. The will (chooser)

4   The unity of soul and body with Spirit; the coming into a right relationship with God comes through Jesus Christ and it comes in the present moment, in the right now.

5. If we are in Christ, the Kingdom of God is within us, right now, at this present moment.

6   God is still in the revealing business. There is the Old Testament, the New Testament and the Now Testament.

7   Jesus came to make the way and show the way for all humankind to come again into a right relationship with God.

-5-

The Sower and the Seed-

As we saw in the introduction to this little book, many people are struggling to discover who they are and where they stand today—in the family, the community and the world. It has been my experience that everyone asks the following six questions:

1. Who is God and what is He really like?
2. Who am I and why am I here?
3. How do I relate to others?
4. What is the will of God for my life?
5. How do I fulfill God's will for my life?
6. What are the benefits?

In the previous four chapters, we have seen that the first four questions are answered by revealed knowledge from God. Once we have received and understand the answers to the first four questions, we invariably seek answers to the last two. The answer to "How do I fulfill God's will for my life?" comes through learning, teaching, and doing. Let's do some learning, teaching, and doing!

The Journey is a teaching ministry. We are disciples of Jesus. A disciple is a learner, or pupil, who endeavors to do what she or he is learning. A teacher is one who teaches the disciple. A teacher, a true teacher, endeavors to do what she or he teaches.

Concerning the teachers and preachers who do not practice what they preach, we are not to do what they do; for they do not practice what they preach. They tie up heavy loads and put them on men's shoulders, but they themselves are not willing to lift a finger to move them. Everything they do is done for men to see. They love the place of honor at banquets and the most important seats in church, perhaps even to have their congregations furnish season tickets to the local sporting event, play, or orchestra.

They love to be greeted in public, as "Reverend", "Pastor", "Preacher", "Apostle", "Bishop", or "Rabbi".

Jesus teaches:

> "But you are not to be called 'Rabbi,' for you have only one Master and you are all brothers [and sisters]. And do not call anyone on earth 'father,' for you have one Father, and he is in heaven. Nor are you to be called 'teacher,' for you have one Teacher, the Christ." (Matthew 23: 8-12; emphasis added)

With every lesson that God delivers through me to *The Journey*, I pray that God hide Dan Henley, God extinguish Dan Henley, God literally destroy anything that is in Dan Henley, and use me as His vessel to deliver His message. **We all only have one Teacher, the Christ!**

Jesus is our Teacher. He practices what He preaches. We are His disciples. We are His learners, or pupils, who endeavor to do what we are learning. Jesus said, "If you hold to my teaching, you are really my disciples. Then you will know the truth, and the truth will set you free" (John

8:31-32). If we hold to His teaching, that is, if we endeavor to do what we are learning, we are really His disciples.

Jesus often taught through parables. The dictionary defines a parable as a simple story illustrating a moral or religious lesson. Indeed, Jesus' teaching is simple; however, it is gloriously profound!

There is one parable to which you should pay particular attention. This is the parable of the sower and the seed. Jesus Himself said concerning this parable, "Don't you understand this parable? How then will you understand any parable?" (Mark 4:13). The understanding of this parable and your endeavoring to do from what you learn will personally unlock the door of the Kingdom for you. You will learn for yourself how you are to fulfill God's will in your life. My understanding of this parable was an "ah-ha" moment for me. The light bulb went on in my head. The key I had been looking a lifetime for had been found. Let's start unlocking some Kingdom doors. Jesus said, "Ask and it will be given to you; seek and you will find; knock and the door will be opened to you. For everyone who asks receives; he who seeks finds; and to him who knocks, the door will be opened" (Matthew 7:7-8).

If you have a Bible, turn to Mark Chapter 4. At *The Journey*, we read God's Word, we listen to God's Word, and we speak God's Word. We let God's Word enter through our eyes, our ears and our mouth gates.

Mark 4: 1-8:

Again Jesus began to teach by the lake. The crowd that gathered around him was so large that he got into a boat and sat in it out on the lake, while all the people were along the shore at the water's edge. He taught them many things by parables, and in his teaching said: "Listen! A farmer went out to sow his seed. As he was scattering the seed, some fell along the path, and the birds came and ate it up. Some fell on rocky places, where it did not have much soil. It sprang up quickly, because the soil was shallow. But when the sun came up, the plants were scorched, and they withered because they had no root. Other seed fell among thorns, which grew up and choked the plants, so that they did not bear grain. Still other seed fell on good soil. It came up, grew and produced a crop, multiplying thirty, sixty, or even a hundred times."

I love to visualize this event. Jesus got in a boat and went out onto the lake. His followers were gathered on the shore. Here is Jesus preaching and teaching from the stage of the boat. His followers were on the shore, in a natural amphitheatre. Jesus, God's perfect revelation of Himself, was preaching amongst the natural creations of God. The message He delivered was awesome!

"Listen!" He said with a capital "L" and an exclamation point. When God says Listen!—capital "L," exclamation point—this is no still small voice. This is a voice, a word of authority, delivered to penetrate hardened and obstinate hearts.

A farmer was sowing or planting seed. As he scattered the seed, it fell either along the path, in rocky places, among thorns or in good soil. The seed only produced a sustained crop when it fell in good soil.

Jesus was asked to explain the parable. His explanation was as follows:

- The farmer sows the Word.

- Some people are like seed along the path, where the Word is sown. As soon as they hear it, Satan comes and takes away the Word that was sown in them.

- Others, like seed sown on rocky places, hear the Word and at once receive it with joy. But since they have no root, they last only a short time. When trouble or persecution comes because of the Word, they quickly fall away.

- Still others, like seed sown among thorns, hear the Word; but the worries of this life, the deceitfulness of wealth and the desires for other things, come in and choke the Word making it unfruitful.

- Others, like seed sown on good soil, hear the Word, accept it, and produce a crop—thirty, sixty or even a hundred times what was sown." (Mark 4: 14-20)

Let's say, the Sower is God and He is sowing His Word, His seed, which is incorruptible and designed to produce His fruit. The Word of God, His seed, is immutable. It never changes. Mathematicians would label it a constant. The constant (God's Word) is multiplied by a variable (the soil, which represents us) to produce fruit. The equation would look like this:

God's Word (seed) X The soil (us) = Good Fruit

The variables in this equation are the nature of the soil. Let's say, the soil is us, it is representative of our souls and bodies. The fruit in the equation is the fruit produced by the seed. All seed has as its exclusive purpose, the production of fruit. Now let's review the parable again in light of our equation.

God's Word, God's seed, is sown and it misses the soil. The bird, Satan, immediately takes it away. Satan's goal is to prevent the soil from receiving the seed, to prevent us from receiving God's Word. There are occasions when I am delivering a message at *The Journey* and there will be a persistent baby crying or a cell phone ringing that will

72

interrupt the message. It is then I know that a mighty seed is being sown because Satan is attempting to take it away. God's Word, snatched away by Satan produces no fruit.

God's Word, God's seed, is sown and it falls on rocky places. We hear the Word and at once receive it with joy. But since our soil is rocky, the seed merely germinates; it has no root and will only last a short time. When trouble or persecution comes because of the Word, we quickly fall away. I see this often.

Attendees at *The Journey* are jumping up and down with joy and enthusiasm! They will say, "Pastor Dan, what an inspiration, what a life changing message!" Then they will return to their corporate worlds on Monday and when confronted about their spiritual walk, their enthusiasm quickly fades. God's Word thrown into rocky soil produces no fruit.

God's Word, God's seed is sown, and it falls among thorns. We hear the Word; but the worries of this life, the deceitfulness of wealth, and the desires for other things, come in and choke the Word making it unfruitful. This is the point at which most of us pupils on our spiritual walks find ourselves. We have plowed and fertilized our soil, our bodies and souls, to make them receptive to the Word of God. The seed germinates and begins to grow but we let the cares and concerns of the world, the deceitfulness of wealth, and the desires for things other than the Word of God, keep us from producing good fruit. God's Word thrown into thorns produces no fruit.

God's Word, God's seed is sown and it falls into good soil. We hear the Word, accept it, and produce a crop multiplying—thirty, sixty or even a hundred times what was sown. God's Word thrown into good soil produces fruit! It produces this fruit **exponentially** and the character of the fruit that is produced is love, joy, peace, patience, kindness, goodness, faithfulness, gentleness and self-control. Once fruit is produced in our character, it then shows up in our actions and in the exceptional and extraordinary results in our lives.

How do we make our soil, our souls and bodies, so that God's seed can be planted in us and we can produce exponentially? We must, by our own free will and self-destination, become good soil; receptive to the seed of God through Jesus Christ and through His instructions regarding prayer, meditation and fasting, hearing God's Word and putting it into practice.

Jesus instructed us to pray as follows:

"And when you pray, do not be like the hypocrites, for they love to pray standing in the synagogues and on the street corners to be seen by men. I tell you the truth, they have received their reward in full. But when you pray, go into your room, close the door and pray to your Father, who is unseen. Then your Father, who sees what is done in secret, will reward you. And when you pray, do not keep on babbling like pagans, for they think they will be heard because of their many words. Do not be like them, for your Father knows what you need before you ask him.

This, then, is how you should pray:

'Our Father in heaven,
hallowed be your name,
your kingdom come,
your will be done

on earth as it is in heaven.

Give us today our daily bread.

Forgive us our debts,

as we also have forgiven our debtors.

And lead us not into temptation,

but deliver us from the evil one.'

For if you forgive men when they sin against you, your heavenly Father will also forgive you. But if you do not forgive men their sins, your Father will not forgive your sins." (Matthew 6: 5-15)

We are to pray that God's Kingdom and His will be done on earth, as it is in heaven. We are not to pray that God make our wants happen or that God's will and purpose for us be as we think they should be.

God's Kingdom is here right now. It is in us right now on this earth. Do you really think if you have not entered the Kingdom of God right here on earth, you can enter God's eternal Kingdom? This is what Jesus was talking about when He said, "Enter through the narrow gate. For wide is the gate and broad is the road that leads to destruction, and many enter through it. But small is the gate and narrow the road that leads to life, and only a few find it" (Matthew 7:13-14).

We need to be so consumed in God through Jesus in this present moment that all concerns and cares of the world are forgotten and our absorption in God is so complete, there is no concern about the ultimate outcome of anything. Our only concern is that God's will be done. But what is God's will? God's will is that we have a right relationship with Him and a right relationship with each other. Jesus said:

"When the Son of Man comes in his glory, and all the angels with him, he will sit on his throne in heavenly glory. All the nations will be gathered before him, and he will separate the people one from another as a shepherd separates the sheep from the goats. He will put the sheep on his right and the goats on his left.

"Then the King will say to those on his right, 'Come, you who are blessed by my Father; take your inheritance, the kingdom prepared for you since the creation of the

77

world. For I was hungry and you gave me something to eat, I was thirsty and you gave me something to drink, I was a stranger and you invited me in, I needed clothes and you clothed me, I was sick and you looked after me, I was in prison and you came to visit me.'

"Then the righteous will answer him, 'Lord, when did we see you hungry and feed you, or thirsty and give you something to drink? When did we see you a stranger and invite you in, or needing clothes and clothe you? When did we see you sick or in prison and go to visit you?'

"The King will reply, 'I tell you the truth, whatever you did for one of the least of these brothers of mine, you did for me.'

"Then he will say to those on his left, 'Depart from me, you who are cursed, into the eternal fire prepared for the devil and his angels. For I was hungry and you gave me nothing to eat, I was thirsty and you gave me nothing to drink, I was a stranger and you did not invite me in, I needed clothes and you did not clothe me, I was sick and in prison and you did not look after me.'

"They also will answer, 'Lord, when did we see you hungry or thirsty or a stranger or needing clothes or sick or in prison, and did not help you?'

"He will reply, 'I tell you the truth, whatever you did not do for one of the least of these, you did not do for me.' Then they will go away to eternal punishment, but the righteous to eternal life." (Matthew 25:31-46)

The key to fulfilling the will of God in our lives is right relationships, first to God and then to each other. Christians think Christianity is a religion. It is not. Christianity is all about relationships. Christianity cannot exist with only one individual. Jesus said that where two or three of us come together in His name, there He will be also (Matthew 18:20).

We have to be watchmen over our good soil. There are many types of seeds. They produce what they are supposed to produce. An apple seed does not produce a pecan tree. There is the seed sown by God, His Word, but there are a

79

multitude of other seeds that produce something less. Many of these seeds are negative and if sown into good soil produce and multiply negatively.

We must always be on guard for false prophets, who attempt to sow seeds of negativity into good soil. Jesus warned that these scoundrels come to us in sheep's clothing but they are in reality ferocious wolves. An elected representative who positions him/herself as a protector of children and sends sleazy e-mails to children is a wolf in sheep's clothing. We can recognize these wolves by the fruit they produce or rather don't produce. These scoundrels don't produce love, joy, peace, patience, kindness, goodness, faithfulness, gentleness and self-control. Rather, they are likely to produce: sexual immorality, impurity, excessive indulgence in sensual pleasures, idolatry, witchcraft, hatred, discord, jealousy, fits of rage, selfish ambition, dissensions, factions, envy, drunkenness, orgies, and the like...racism, sexism, chauvinism, national xenophobia, and all other evils, which are in opposition to God.

As watchmen, we must be certain that no one is allowed to sow negative seeds into the good soil of our children. Jesus said, "And whoever welcomes a little child like this in my name welcomes me. But if anyone causes one of these little ones who believe in me to sin, it would be better for him to have a large millstone hung around his neck and to be drowned in the depths of the sea" (Matthew 18:5-6).

Biblical quotations and references are sprinkled throughout this book. I urge you for the next 21 days to make these references yours. Pray and meditate on these for the next 21 days. Quiet your minds and listen to the still, small voice.

I pray for you to recognize, as did Paul of Tarsus:

You were dead in your sin.

You used to live and follow the ways of the world, the ways of Satan, who is still at work in those who are disobedient.

You used to gratify the cravings of a sinful nature, worshiping false gods.

81

When I think about Satan and his myriad of tricks, I try to put them into a framework that is simple in my mind. For instance, temptation is just like a person who is applying for a job. The person responsible for hiring the position will either accept or decline the application. Temptation is no different. When Satan tempts us, he is applying for an opportunity to work in our lives. We have the choice to either accept or decline his application. Satan will continue to tempt both the obedient and the disobedient; however, it is only in the disobedient that he finds his full time employment.

> ... But because of his great love for us, God, who is rich in mercy, made us alive with Christ even when we were dead in transgressions—it is by grace you have been saved. And God raised us up with Christ and seated us with him in the heavenly realms in Christ Jesus, in order that in the coming ages he might show the incomparable riches of his grace, expressed in his kindness to us in Christ Jesus. For it is by grace you have been saved, through faith—and this not from yourselves, it is the gift of God—

not by works, so that no one can boast. For we are God's workmanship, created in Christ Jesus to do good works, which God prepared in advance for us to do.(Ephesians 2:4-10)

Those on this journey need spiritual models. We must seek and identify others who are traveling in Spirit on this journey. I don't mean Biblical scholars and theologians, but men and women who act based upon intuition, conscience, and the spark of God, rather than through their emotions and feelings through what they were born with, what they were taught, what they have learned, and their life experiences. God knows and speaks their names and they experience divine revelations.

We must observe the actions and positions advocated by any potential model. We must be aware of the ferocious wolves in sheep's clothing. A spiritual model's actions will be based upon love, joy, peace, patience, kindness, goodness, faithfulness, gentleness, and self-control.

The positions advocated by a spiritual model will be based upon the teachings of Jesus, not the laws and traditions of man. They will not advocate positions in opposition to God such as racism, sexism, male chauvinism, or national xenophobia. They will advocate positions based upon love (nature of God) rather than fear (nature of Satan). Therefore:

They will not, in the name of Jesus, advocate that blacks be thrown into the cargo holes of slave ships.

They will not, in the name of Jesus, advocate that Jews be tossed into gas chambers. They will not, in the name of Jesus, advocate that homosexuals be treated like less than human beings. They will recognize that homosexuals, as are all human beings, are the children of God.

They will not, in the name of Jesus, advocate that preemptive wars of national hegemony be conducted, killing tens of thousands of innocent people.

They will not, in the name of Jesus, advocate that education at prestigious universities only be available for the few, while the many barely receive high school diplomas.

They will not, in the name of Jesus, advocate that state of the art medical care be available for only a select few.

They will not, in the name of Jesus, advocate that an American aristocracy be perpetuated, while a large percentage of the country lives in poverty.

They will not, in the name of Jesus, advocate that taxes are a burden imposed by the state, rather they understand that a tax is an investment in the country. Jesus taught a viable and prosperous country is necessary for His Church to prosper. "Give to Caesar what is Caesar's, and to God what is God's" (Matthew 22:21).

They will not, in the name of Jesus, advocate that the earth be raped and pillaged, rather they understand that with man and woman's dominion over the earth comes the responsibility for the earth's welfare. To rape and pillage the earth is like urinating on the streets of heaven.

As Jesus said:

"Whoever can be trusted with very little can also be trusted with much, and whoever is dishonest with very little will also be dishonest with much. So if you have not been trustworthy in handling worldly wealth, who will trust you with true riches? And if you have not been trustworthy with someone else's property, who will give you property of your own?" (Luke 16: 10-12)

If we cannot act responsibly and honestly with the earth, God's creation, God's property, over which we have been designated as stewards, God will not give us property of our own. We will not have a parcel in the Kingdom of God. Instead of earthly wealth, we are to seek spiritual wealth. As Jesus taught, "But seek first his kingdom and his righteousness, and all these things will be given to you as well" (Matthew 6:33).

At *The Journey* we occasionally participate in media fasts. For 21 days, we leave all media alone. We are mindful of what enters through our eye and ear gates. We don't watch television and we don't listen to radios, CDs or entertainment tapes. We only read printed matter of a spiritual nature. Over the next 21 days as you pray and meditate on the scriptures quoted in this little book, if you also fast from the media, you will begin to understand how you are to fulfill God's will in your own life.

Once you have this understanding, actively seek out spiritual models that are also traveling on this spiritual journey. Pay attention to the actions of these models. Talk to them, question them, and emulate them. Strive to be so consumed in God through Jesus in the present moment that all of your concerns and cares of the world are forgotten. Let your absorption in God be so complete that you have no concerns about the ultimate outcome of anything. Let your only concern be that God's will be done in your life.

Ω

Empowering Right Relationships:
First to God, Then to Each Other

Principles:

1. A disciple is a learner, or pupil, who endeavors to do what she or he is learning.

2. A true teacher is one who teaches the disciple and endeavors to do what she or he teaches.

3. Understanding and endeavoring to do what you learn of the parable of the Sower and the seed unlocks the door to the riches of the Kingdom of God.

4. The Sower is God and He is sowing His Word, His seed. His Word is incorruptible and designed to produce His fruit in our lives.

5. We are the soil. The soil represents our souls and our bodies.

6. God's Word(seed) X The soil(us) = Good Fruit

7. The key to the Kingdom of God is right relationships; first to God and then to each other.

8. Christianity is not a religion. It is all about relationships.

9. We have to become watchmen over our good soil and over our children.

-6-

Spiritual Wealth-

Once we understand how we are to fulfill God's will in each of our lives and act upon this understanding, the benefits to each of us are enormous. We are rewarded with spiritual wealth. Jesus described it in this manner:

> When a Samaritan woman came to draw water, Jesus said to her, "Will you give me a drink?" (His disciples had gone into the town to buy food.)
>
> The Samaritan woman said to him, "You are a Jew and I am a Samaritan woman. How can you ask me for a drink?" (For Jews do not associate with Samaritans.)
>
> Jesus answered her, "If you knew the gift of God and who it is that asks you for a drink, you would have asked him and he would have given you living water."

"Sir," the woman said, "you have nothing to draw with and the well is deep. Where can you get this living water? Are you greater than our father Jacob, who gave us the well and drank from it himself, as did also his sons and his flocks and herds?"

Jesus answered, "Everyone who drinks this water will be thirsty again, but whoever drinks the water I give him will never thirst. Indeed, the water I give him will become in him a spring of water welling up to eternal life."

The woman said to him, "Sir, give me this water so that I won't get thirsty and have to keep coming here to draw water." (John 4: 7-15)

Similarly, there was a television game show where at the end of the program the winner of the game opened one of three doors and kept whatever was behind the door. The winner did not know what was behind any of the three doors before they were opened. Our lives on earth, in these earth suits, are much like this, except we know what is behind the three doors before we open them.

You have your free will and self-destination to open and step through any of the three doors. Behind the first door is a mirror. It reflects you in your earth suit and what you have been taught, and what you have learned through your life experiences. This is as good as it gets.

Behind the second door are all of the riches of the world; the riches to be gained by adhering to man's law and traditions and worshiping false gods. If you open and step through this second door, it comes with a caveat. "What good will it be for a man if he gains the whole world, yet forfeits his soul? Or what can a man give in exchange for his soul?" (Matthew 18:26).

To open the third door, the door to the Kingdom of God, you must give up everything you possess. Jesus said, "If anyone would come after me, he must deny himself and take up his cross and follow me" (Matthew 18: 24). Your opening and stepping through this door is the convergence of heaven and earth. God connects with you on earth, kisses you paternally on the forehead, and fills your vessel with His seed, His blessing, and His riches—the true riches.

Once we have God's seed, God's blessing, and the true riches, what do we do with them? We have seen that worldly people are shrewd. They know how to use money to open worldly doors of opportunity for themselves.

As a businessman, I drove the largest Mercedes Benz car, wore fine clothes, and mingled with the right people. I would make significant contributions to the most prestigious charities of the rich and was ultimately rewarded with worldly wealth. I had opened and stepped through the second door by being shrewd and adhering to worldly ways.

You recall Jesus' parable of the shrewd manager. Jesus explained it as:

> "Whoever can be trusted with very little can also be trusted with much, and whoever is dishonest with very little will also be dishonest with much. So if you have not been trustworthy in handling worldly wealth, who will trust you with true riches? And if you have not been trustworthy with someone else's property, who will give you property of your own?
>
> No servant can serve two masters. Either he will hate the one and love the other, or he will

be devoted to the one and despise the other. You cannot serve both God and Money." (Luke 16:10-13)

When the Pharisees, members of a Jewish sect that emphasized strict interpretation and observance of the Mosaic law in both its oral and written form, and who were hypocritically self-righteous and who loved money, heard all this and were sneering at Jesus, He said to them, "You are the ones who justify yourselves in the eyes of men, but God knows your hearts. What is highly valued among men is detestable in God's sight" (Luke 16:14-15).

We know we are to sow God's seed, God's blessing (the true riches) into good soil and fruit will be produced exponentially. This is our purpose. As was described by Jesus in the parable of the talents:

"Again, it will be like a man going on a journey, who called his servants and entrusted his property to them. To one he gave five talents of money, to another two talents, and to another one talent, each according to his ability. Then he went on his journey. The man who had received the five talents went at once and put his money to work and gained five more. So also, the one with the two talents gained two more. But the man who had received the one talent went off, dug a hole in the ground and hid his master's money.

After a long time the master of those servants returned and settled accounts with them. The man who had received the five talents brought the other five. 'Master,' he said, 'you entrusted me with five talents. See, I have gained five more.'

His master replied, 'Well done, good and faithful servant! You have been faithful with a few things; I will put you in charge of many things. Come and share your master's happiness!'

The man with the two talents also came. 'Master,' he said, 'you entrusted me with two talents; see, I have gained two more.'

His master replied, 'Well done, good and faithful servant! You have been faithful with a few things; I will put you in charge of many things. Come and share your master's happiness!'

Then the man who had received the one talent came. 'Master,' he said, 'I knew that you are a hard man, harvesting where you have not sown and gathering where you have not scattered seed. So I was afraid and went out and hid your talent in the ground. See, here is what belongs to you.'

"His master replied, 'You wicked, lazy servant! So you knew that I harvest where I have not sown and gather where I have not scattered seed? Well then, you should have put my money on deposit with the bankers, so that when I returned I would have received it back with interest.

'Take the talent from him and give it to the one who has the ten talents. For everyone who has will be given more, and he will have an abundance. Whoever does not have, even what he has will be taken from him. And throw that worthless servant outside, into the darkness,

97

where there will be weeping and gnashing of teeth." (Matthew 25:14-28)

We are to invest what has been entrusted to us; our time, our talents, and our resources into what's valuable to God. We are not to invest in what is valued by man because what is valuable to man is detestable to God. We must understand what is valuable to God.

Let's say you are reading this book on an airplane. What is around you? Airline seats, luggage, a serving cart, newspapers, books, magazines, pens, pencils, electronic games, laptop computers, blankets, pillows, and other people on the plane are some of the things that surround you. Which of these things are valuable to God? You and the other people are valuable to God.

We need to understand that God is not opposed to us having money. In Jesus' original group of twelve, some owned successful fishing companies and one was a highly compensated government official. One of the disciples was even appointed treasurer over their finances. A treasurer was needed because they had discussions over how to distribute the monies. Do not say, "My power and the strength of my hands have produced this wealth for me." But remember the LORD your God, for it is he who gives you the ability to produce wealth (Deuteronomy 8:17-18). God has given us the ability to produce wealth, to make money. Money is itself not evil. Indeed it is neither good nor evil but is neutral. What matters is where you invest this money.

Paul of Tarsus observed:

"If anyone teaches false doctrines and does not agree to the sound instruction of our Lord Jesus Christ and to godly teaching, he is conceited and understands nothing. He has an unhealthy interest in controversies and quarrels about words that result in envy, strife, malicious talk, evil suspicions and constant friction between men of corrupt mind, who have been robbed of the truth and who think that godliness is a means to financial gain.

But godliness with contentment is great gain. For we brought nothing into the world, and we can take nothing out of it. But if we have food and clothing, we will be content

99

with that. People who want to get rich fall into temptation and a trap and into many foolish and harmful desires that plunge men into ruin and destruction. For the love of money is a root of all kinds of evil. Some people, eager for money, have wandered from the faith and pierced themselves with many griefs." (I Timothy 6:3-10)

It is the love of money and how it can seduce you away from a right relationship with God that is evil. It is taking money and investing it in what is detestable to God that is evil. We must invest in what is valuable to God: people, lost sheep, lost souls. In Romans 12:2, Paul conveys to us that our spiritual act of worship is to offer our bodies as living sacrifices. As recipients of God's anointing, God's blessing, we are tasked with giving them away, by allowing God to use our lives to be a blessing to others. God's blessings are eternal and never ending. It is like a spring which never stops running, the well which never runs dry. Everyone who has and invests in bringing people into right relationships with God and each other will be given more and will have abundance.

Experts concerning man's laws and traditions were complaining of Jesus, "This man welcomes sinners and eats with them." Jesus responded to them with a parable, explaining why we must reach out to sinners. We must reach out to those who are deliberately disobeying the known will of God. We must reach out and give a blessing to those who are estranged from God because of their disobedience. Jesus said:

"Suppose one of you has a hundred sheep and loses one of them. Does he not leave the ninety-nine in the open country and go after the lost sheep until he finds it? And when he finds it, he joyfully puts it on his shoulders and goes home. Then he calls his friends and neighbors together and says, 'Rejoice with me; I have found my lost sheep. **I tell you that in the same way there will be more rejoicing in heaven over one sinner who repents than over ninety-nine righteous persons who do not need to repent.**" (Luke 15: 4-7)

101

The nature of God is Love. He wants us all to be in a right relationship with Him and with each other. As we have been blessed with an anointing, we are to share this, give it away, and sow it. Sow it into good soil so that it multiplies thirty, sixty, or even a hundred times. This is our task. This is our purpose. We are the hands of God on this earth.

We must also remember that whatever we sow, we will also reap. So as we begin to sow into good soil, we need to stop placing obstacles in the way of our blessings. You recall the parable of the Sower and the seed. You remember that God's Word, God's seed is sown, and some of it falls among thorns. We hear the Word; but the worries of this life, the deceitfulness of wealth, and the desires for other things come in and choke the Word, making it unfruitful.

This is the point at which most of us on this spiritual walk find ourselves. We have plowed and fertilized our soil, our bodies and souls, to make them receptive to the Word of God. The seed germinates and begins to grow; but, we let the cares of the world, the deceitfulness of wealth and the desires for things other than the Word, keep us from producing fruit. The cares and concerns of this world (our worries) prevent us from receiving our full blessings.

Jesus instructed us not to worry. If we receive an instruction from Jesus and we do not follow it, we are deliberately disobeying the known will of God. He told us, "Do not worry about your life, what you will eat or drink; or about your body, what you will wear. Is not life more important than food, and the body more important than clothes?" (Matthew 6:25).

Yet we worry about paying our bills, providing for our children's educations, our health, our safety, our jobs, and on and on. This is because we are three-part beings. We function in Spirit, soul, and body simultaneously. To receive our full blessings we must totally repudiate our souls and bodies. To repudiate means to reject as having no authority or binding force. So likewise, we must continue to think, but not be mastered by our thinking. We must continue to feel and not be controlled by our feelings. Yes, we will continue to have desires; however, we will not be subjected to, or enslaved by, our desires. On the contrary, our thinking, our feelings, and our desires will be submitted to Christ who lives inside of us.

Only Christ could live like this completely and all the time and we are not Christ. But we should follow His Way and strive to be perfect as He is perfect. We need to stop worrying and trust God that His will and His Kingdom will be done on earth, as it is in heaven. Be mindful of what Jesus taught, "Look at the birds of the air; they do not sow or reap or store away in barns, and yet your heavenly Father feeds them. Are you not much more valuable than they? Who of you by worrying can add a single hour to his life?" (Matthew 6:26-27).

You cannot add an hour to your life through worry. Observe what Jesus says is valuable. ***It is people—it is you!*** Let's begin to invest now in God's people, without worry, without any attachment to the outcome of God's ultimate plan.

You can begin this by identifying a Christian Reconciliation Church such as *The Journey*. Find a church that is listening to God's Word and putting it into practice. Find a church which is teaching the Word of God, not the laws and traditions of man. Find a

church that is doing as Jesus taught: "Love the Lord your God with all your heart and with all your soul and with all your mind. This is the first and greatest commandment. And the second is like it: Love your neighbor as yourself." Begin to invest in this church. Invest your time, your energies, your monies, your Spirit, souls, and bodies. Make a commitment to tithe into this church right now. Make a commitment to sow the seeds, to give the blessings away, for everyone who has and invests in bringing people into right relationships with God and each other will be given more and will have abundance.

When you stop obsessing about earthly wealth and dedicate your life to the will of God, you need not ask "What are the benefits?" You will acquire the freedom that comes from living in Truth—God's standard of what is right. You will know the joy of sharing God's message and love to others. You will be excited to be used as a vessel to demonstrate His glory in your life.

You will know that He is your bread of life and your living water that fills every empty spot in your life. You will know that, as a believer, you share eternal life in His Kingdom both now and forever more!

Ω

Empowering Right Relationships:
First to God, Then to Each Other

Principles:

1   God connects with you on earth, kisses you paternally on the forehead and fills your vessel with His seeds, blessings and true riches.

2   Money is itself not evil. Indeed money is neither good nor evil but is neutral. What matters is where you invest this money.

3   We must invest in what is valuable to God—people, lost sheep, lost souls.

4. Everyone who has and invests in bringing people into right relationships with God and each other will be given more and will have abundance.

5. We need to stop worrying and trust God.

6. Let's begin to invest *now* in God's people, without worry and without attachment to the outcome of God's ultimate plan.

7. Identify a Christian Reconciliation Church, such as *The Journey Church*, and invest your tithe (10%), your energies, your monies, your Spirit, souls, and bodies.

A Final Prayer-

Dear Father in heaven,

We just stop to say "thank You." Thank You for Your blessing. Thank You for the blessings we see every day and also for the ones that we are totally unaware of. Thank You for sending Your Son, and our big brother, Jesus, to be a model for us. Now let us live a life that is pleasing and acceptable to You by us learning to value what You value and that is people. Thank You for sending Your precious Holy Spirit to guide us into right relationships with You and with each other. In Jesus' name we pray.

Amen.

Appendix-

Chapter 1: Nature of God

Page 11:

> The Ten Commandments can be found in Exodus, Chapter 20.

Chapter 3: Borders

Page 35

> The story of Abel is found in Genesis, Chapter 4.
>
> The story of Enoch is found in Genesis, Chapters 4 and 5.
>
> The story of Noah is found in Genesis, Chapters 5 through 9.
>
> The story of Abraham and Sarah is found in Genesis, Chapters 11 through 25.

Page 36:

> The story of Isaac is found in Genesis, Chapters 17 through 28.
>
> The story of Jacob is found in Genesis, Chapters 25 through 50.

The story of Joseph is found in Genesis, Chapters 30 through 50.

The story of Moses is found in the book of Exodus.

Page 37:

The story of Rahab is found in Joshua, Chapters 2 through 6.

www.ingramcontent.com/pod-product-compliance
Lightning Source LLC
LaVergne TN
LVHW021354080426
835508LV00020B/2278